THE
WISDOM
TRAIL GUIDE

31 STEPS TO A LIFE OF WISDOM

NATHAN KING

THE WISDOM TRAIL GUIDE:

31 STEPS TO A LIFE OF WISDOM

Copyright © 2021, Nathan King

Published by Nathan King

Cover design by Nathan King

Edited by Pat Taylor

ISBN: 978-1-7374691-2-4

EBOOK ISBN: 978-1-7374691-0-0

To Jamie. Every trail is better with you.

WELCOME TO THE TRAILHEAD

I stood there just staring ahead with a big decision to make. I'm sure the importance of my pending choice was etched upon my face like a warrior choosing his weapon. This decision would set the course of my life for the foreseeable future. The weighty decision pressed down on me. I could feel my kids gathered behind me anticipating the outcome of this life-changing decision. Finally, it was time. "I'll take three cups of chocolate with sprinkles and hot fudge please." Whew, that was a close one.

Obviously, my choice of ice cream on an afternoon outing with my kids doesn't carry the weight of the kingdom. But you and I make weighty decisions all the time. Sometimes they are overt decisions like whether to switch jobs, move to a new home, or make some other life altering change. Other decisions are subtle. They are the habits we carve out one choice at a time; in the way we spend our moments, consume our entertainment, or talk with friends.

Nothing we do is wasted. All of it matters—it shapes who we are. Do you know what no one has ever said to me? "Wow, I hope I am not a wise person." I've never received a text that read, "I just made a really huge decision and I hope it was the wrong one." That has never happened.

On the flip side, it seems like someone reaches out to me every day needing help with a decision. They are facing a choice. They come in search of a friendly voice. Someone willing and able to offer counsel. Someone who will point them down the trail.

Once upon a time I was really afraid of letting people down. Now, many years later, I know letting people down kind of comes with breathing. We disappoint each other all the time. That's not me being cynical. That's called honesty.

Do you know what would really let my friends down when they look for help? If I offer empty platitudes rather than earned Wisdom. So that's precisely what I try to serve up; Wisdom.

Let me be really clear about something that won't surprise you. It's something my Mom, my wife, and a great many others learned a long time ago. I frequently falter where Wisdom is concerned. I don't have Wisdom penned up in my backyard where I go to collect some whenever I have a need. That would be wonderful; But weird. Wisdom doesn't work that way. There aren't any tricks. There are no shortcuts to Wisdom.

There isn't a Wisdom Genie you can carry around in your pocket. You can't throw a coin into the Wisdom Well. You can't attain Wisdom wishing upon a star. No pots of Wisdom are waiting at the end of the rainbow. No Wisdom is to be had if you manage to chase down a unicorn.

Wisdom isn't a miracle. Wisdom is earned. Wisdom is harvested one hard turn of the soil at a time. You acquire wisdom across a lifetime of trial and error. Good luck. I laughed when I wrote that because it sounds so fatalistic.

Wisdom isn't quite that hard to get. It's not magic, but it's not the secret prize waiting at the end of the Hunger Games either.

There is a path to Wisdom. Sometimes it's a clear next step on a well-trodden trail. Sometimes it's a bushwhack through the jungle. Either way it is worth it because Wisdom is amazing. It calls to us from across human history. We can find it in poetry. We can sit at the feet of our elders and learn many lessons. Wisdom is incredible.

It's no small wonder that God put Wisdom on the hearts of the many men who wrote what would come to be known as the Bible. In fact, right in the heart of the book many people call the "Word of God" is what is also fondly referred to as the "Wisdom Literature". That's no accident.

Wisdom will guard your heart from many things. But it will guard your head, your home, your wallet, and your well-being too.

Sometimes when I talk to people about Wisdom they get this look in their eyes like it's too hard a thing to chase down. As if the pursuit of Wisdom is some grandiose quest God dangles in front of us like a carrot on a stick. Look, when it comes to God there are no carrots and there are no sticks. There's just a really great Dad who loves his kids and wants what's best for them.

Wisdom is not something God wants from you. Wisdom is something God wants FOR you.

In the heart of the Wisdom Literature is a small book that captures the culture of an ancient people led by wise kings. That's not something to be balked at. This small book of thirty one short chapters holds the collective Wisdom of a kingdom that has long fascinated the world. And for good reason.

Have you ever found yourself facing a decision only to wonder, "what is the wise thing here?" Most of us have.

Still, plenty of decisions are made with little regard for Wisdom. In fact I often sit and scratch my head wondering at whether or not we have decided to ditch Wisdom altogether!

The stories of the Bible show us that ancient people did the same thing. They routinely walked away from Wisdom. They made other choices. And their path suffered for it.

Wisdom carries weight, and it opens opportunities. The effects of wise living shape the world before you in so many ways; Even as the effect it has on your personal well-being shapes you for your own good and the betterment of others.

It would be a shame to leave Wisdom on the table. Instead, what if we leaned in when another shot at Wisdom showed up? What if we treated Wisdom like an old friend? What if we could sit at the feet of Wisdom and catch something wonderful? We can.

While becoming wise is not an overnight event or a one-off magic moment, it is a process that you can both invite yourself into and initiate. God made it possible one statement at a time all through the Proverbs.

What is a proverb? It's a short saying packed with significance. And the Book of Proverbs is a collection of them unlike anything else in human history.

Over the next thirty one days I hope you will lean in to see what Wisdom has to say. Remember that it's not asking anything of you. Rather it wants something amazing for you. A life of wisdom is better than you can begin to imagine.

Wisdom leads us toward God. It brings about a unique sense of how to live. It provides order for how to follow and direction for where to go next. Wisdom cuts off the effect of chaos and invites us into a life that bears the remarkable stamp of someone in pursuit of God's best life for them.

This short book is not exhaustive. You won't look up at the end and say, "I've arrived at Wisdom." But hopefully you'll look up after these next steps together and realize you're off to a great start.

Everyday together is meant to cultivate another step forward. I've written short segments I hope will encourage your heart, your head, and your hands as you set off to see what Wisdom has for you.

I hope you won't just read it. Information offers us almost nothing until we do something with it. So each daily entry comes with a challenge. Sometimes the step I'm asking you to take is one you'll do internally. Wisdom has to have a place to reside. You'll work that in prayer and patience as you reflect on the thought of the day. There are also moments when I challenge you to get out into your world and do something. Both are vital.

As you put it all together you will feel yourself moving. It will seem a small thing if this is all new to you. Don't be discouraged. Just keep going. If you miss a day don't beat yourself up. Just don't miss two.

If you really want to squeeze the trail for everything on offer, gather in the company of some good friends and take the journey together. There are questions at the end of each week to guide a group discussion. I can't wait to sit around a campfire someday and find out what you've learned.

BASECAMP

DAY 1

Start with God —the first step in learning is bowing down to God; only fools thumb their noses at such wisdom and learning. (Proverbs 1:7 MSG)

Every good trip starts with a sense of anticipation. Where you're going is always exciting and who you're going with is usually even better. But you can't go if you don't move. You have to begin. The first step down the trail. The first mile on the freeway. You won't go anywhere if you don't start moving.

Today, as we start this month-long pursuit of Wisdom, let us do it with a sense of anticipation. The kind that allows us to approach God with a sense of wonder. Keep in anticipation with a humility that recognizes why you're pursuing Wisdom in the first place.

We don't have all the answers. And the ones we do have we probably didn't come to easily. Isn't that why we started this journey toward Wisdom in the first place?

The wonderful thing about Wisdom is that it always takes us toward God. Why? Because life has a sense of order and direction to it. The order is simple—follow God. When you make a life out of following God the direction he wants for your life becomes a habit, and you move toward him.

Wisdom is not something God wants to squeeze out of you. Wisdom is something God wants for you. Where do we find it? In the places and spaces where we're following him. So just keep going. And if it's been rocky so far don't sweat the small stuff. You are the delight of a really big God.

CHALLENGE: Write down an area of your life where you have made a recent mistake.

Lord, let my heart be open to your wonder. I want to learn from you. Teach me like the good Father you are. Let me be open to correction where I need it. Let me keep taking steps that follow you.

DAY 2

Follow the steps of good men instead, and stay on the paths of the righteous. (Proverbs 2:20 NLT)

My family loves to go on adventures. We hike through the wild places of the mountains in pursuit of time together. We take in the untamed beauty of our natural surroundings. But we don't have to blaze the trail.

I don't hand my four year old a machete at the start of each new hike and say, "Okay, Matt. If we're going to make it to the waterfall today I'm going to need you to cut a path through the trees." That would be crazy.

Instead, we walk on the path carved by the ones who have gone before. Just as they tread trails laid down by someone with a desire to get somewhere.

The order and direction Wisdom invites us into isn't a lonely adventure. Does that mean we'll always be surrounded by crowds? Of course not. Does that mean we have to figure it out all by ourselves? Thankfully, no.

We've all got someone we can get behind. Someone that will help guide us toward the right path. The next step toward Wisdom is making sure you're following the steps of the good guys.

Today, take a good look at your everyday world. Who is going where you want to go? Who is living a life filled to the brim with Wisdom? Don't make it weird; but ask them what it would take to tag along.

Following good steps sets a good pace, a good direction, and a great example. Aim your life at it and you'll wind up where Wisdom wants you.

CHALLENGE: Write down the names of the people that have had the most impact on your life. Is there someone you should add to the list for your next steps down the road to Wisdom?

Lord, I pray that my passionate pursuit of You would keep me on the right path. Help me walk toward You. Help me avoid being self-centered. Thank you so much for pointing me toward people I can follow toward You.

DAY 3

Let not steadfast love and faithfulness forsake you; bind them around your neck; write them on the tablet of your heart. (Proverbs 3:3 ESV)

At the beginning of every year my friend Mark walks into my office and asks the same question, "Nate, what are you dreaming for this year?"

And every year my answer is the same, "Mark, I just want to be faithful." It's not a cop out, even if it isn't exactly the answer he came looking for. As my friend and mentor he is interested in hearing what kind of audacious goal I have in my sights. As a husband, dad, teacher, and pastor, faithfulness is the biggest one I can think of.

Living a life full of Wisdom is no easy task. It seems like there are more obstacles than on-ramps most days. Wisdom is what sets us up for success. Once you've decided to move in the direction of Wisdom you just need steady love and faithfulness.

There will be times when we feel like failures, or are not feeling particularly faithful. Those are the moments when you have to lean past your feelings. Does it seem like you missed it today? Look at what you brought with you. Steadfast love and faithfulness are still hanging on. Don't forget the failing, and don't ignore it, just lean past it into the places where your heart has been changed. That's the spot where Wisdom has etched love and faithfulness into the bedrock of your soul.

Live from the deep well of love and faithfulness that continually moves you forward. Trust in the goodness of God.

Good luck being perfect. Only Jesus ever pulled that off. Instead measure up to steadfast love and faithfulness. The consistency of those overwhelming forces invited into your daily life will be a welcome presence as you move down the path where Wisdom is leading you.

The next time you're facing an uncertain choice ask this question: where is love and faithfulness leading me?

CHALLENGE: Write the words "love" and "faithfulness" on a notecard and stick it in your pocket. Or put them on the background of your phone. The next time you have to make a decision, look at those words. Where are they guiding you?

Father, when I am not feeling particularly good, loving, or faithful; that is when I most need You to make up the difference. Continue to shape my heart so that if that day should come, I can lean into You rather than rely on my own ways.

DAY 4

But the path of the righteous is like the light of dawn, which shines brighter and brighter until full day. (Proverbs 4:18 ESV)

Every winter Jamie and I go with a group of our friends to a nearby lodge. The lodge sits nestled on top of one of the tallest mountains between the Rockies and the Appalachians. Watching dawn break over the valley below is marvelous. As the vast array of early morning color breaks through, it paints the landscape below in a kaleidoscope of light and wonder. It's breathtaking.

When we first begin paying attention to Wisdom it can be quite a bit like dawn breaking over our lives. Suddenly we see things we didn't see before. The landscape of our decisions looks a bit different. Our motivations seemed to be colored anew. It's a wonderful, and sometimes intimidating, experience.

The great thing about allowing Wisdom to lead you down the right path is the further you go the better you can see. Not because life stops throwing you curves or suddenly removes all of its mystery. If anything pursuing the path

God wants for you may take you toward even more winding roads and mysterious invitations.

With each step down the right path we leave behind our murky past and embark on a new adventure. One where Wisdom leads, good friends tag along, and God himself is cheering you ever onward. With each step old failures and mistakes are left further and further behind. With each step Wisdom lights up your life, perspective opens wide before and behind.

Wisdom lets you see where you're going. And it reminds you to be thankful you're no longer where you were.

CHALLENGE: What new thing have you learned about yourself since beginning your journey toward Wisdom?

Jesus, thank You. Through You I am made new. Through You I have found the right path. Through You I'm leaving behind a failing shadow. I am seeing new things about this life you're leading me into.

DAY 5

Mark well that God doesn't miss a move you make; he's aware of every step you take. (Proverbs 5:21 MSG)

When each of my kids were learning to walk it was the highlight of my day to watch them work it out. All four of them were different in the way they approached it. A couple of them learned to crawl, and then pull up, and then took their first daring steps. One of them skipped crawling altogether and just attempted a few wobbly steps.

If I wasn't in the room when one of them was about to give walking a shot Jamie would call to me, and vice versa. Why? Because we didn't want to miss a step.

God doesn't miss a move you make. He doesn't miss a step. Perhaps that makes you a bit uncomfortable. I get it. I don't always make the right moves. Not every step I take is one to be proud of. More than a few of them happen on wobbly legs, and uncertain feet.

The great thing about Wisdom is that it's not an exercise in perfect expectations. Yes, you will trip up. Of course you're going to stumble. And it might seem intimidating beyond measure that God himself has his eye on you when your feet get the best of you. Like a loving Father He runs to the room to see what happens next.

Be encouraged. God's not watching because he's hoping you'll fail. He's cheering every courageous attempt. He lovingly guides us toward the right path. He lights it up with Wisdom. He motivates us with love. He strengthens us through our faithfulness with every attempt.

Today, take a new step. It doesn't have to be a big step. Just the next step. Open your heart to the warmth of God watching. Don't get nervous about it. Just get moving.

CHALLENGE: What new thing will you try today?

God, your grace shines on my life as you lead me toward Wisdom. Thank you for what I've learned with every stumble. Thank you for smiling on me with every attempt. Be with me today as I take my next new step.

DAY 6

Go to the ant, O sluggard; consider her ways, and be wise. (Proverbs 6:6 ESV)

My son Matt loves to watch bugs. One day he was enthralled by a colony of ants. He picked one out, called it Anty and acted like he was following it around for most of an afternoon. He watched Anty as he carried a leaf, put it in his hole, and came back for another and another. Anty was taking care of business.

What business do you and I have to take care of? It might actually be business if you're a professional. It could be the business of making your home be all you want it to be. Maybe your business is the nonprofit you lead, the grades you're aiming for, or your next step in a personal goal.

Whatever it is, give yourself over to the big thing we can learn from Matt's friend Anty. Just move. Pick up what you need and take it where it's needed. It could be an idea. Maybe it's an email you've put off sending for too long.

Perhaps it's a pile of boxes your wife has been begging you to take to the garage. Whatever it is, don't put it off.

Wisdom never procrastinates. I know. I know. This one hurts a bit. Why do today what you can put off till tomorrow, right? It's the pattern so many live by. I've had my moments where putting things off was second nature.

Embracing the ever present reality of work is the wise thing. Whatever stage of life, whatever occupation, whatever location, we show Wisdom by applying ourselves and working hard. Giving everything our best not only demonstrates great Wisdom, it also makes a big statement in our life about God. Embracing Wisdom means embracing work.

CHALLENGE: What have you been putting off? Today is the day to get it done. Go for it.

Father, I am going to give today my very best. I want to honor you with my work. Not because it makes you love me, but because I love you. I want the way I approach my work point to your goodness at work in my own life as you lead down the Path of Wisdom.

DAY 7

Do what I say and you'll live well. My teaching is as precious as your eyesight—guard it! (Proverbs 7:2 MSG)

One day Jamie and I took the kids on a winding hike high in the mountains that ended in a cave. We didn't tell them about the amazing surprise waiting for us nestled in the far corner of the cold dark enclosure. The further we squeezed and crawled into the dark recesses the louder the tell-tale sign of the surprise became. Finally, I asked my boys, "What do you think is making that sound?" They didn't have a clue.

Once we made it to the final chamber of the cavern everything opened up. The boys and I breathed a sigh of relief as they gathered in close. I gave them really clear instructions, "boys, everyone put a hand on my arm so you will know how close we are." As soon as I felt the last small grip take hold I shut off the light. They gasped in unison at the abject blackness of a dark the three of them had never before experienced. Because I'm not a jerk I didn't leave them in the dark but for a few short seconds. When I did turn the bright light back on everything seemed brighter—especially the twenty foot waterfall cascading through the cave ceiling.

God shines his words on Wisdom. He points them there in the hope we will follow his lead. Why? He wants us close. He knows the best part of life comes in the wake of what he has to say to us. God's words aren't stifling rules, they're a treasured guide. When we hold them close and follow them true there's no better way to see where to go.

CHALLENGE: Take 5-10 minutes and attempt to do some mundane chore blindfolded or with your eyes closed. How difficult was it? Doing life without Wisdom is kind of like that.

Lord, let me follow close. Let your words be the center of my decision making, conduct, and priorities. I want to live well.

CAMPFIRE CHAT

What stuck out to you this week?

What are you most excited about?

What are you most concerned about?

What was the most challenging part?

What felt easy?

Where did you feel like God gave you strength for the next step?

Where did you need the help of a friend?

Where did you lend someone else a hand?

Are you being honest with yourself so far?

What are you looking forward to?

FIELD NOTES

_____

_____

_____

_____

_____

_____

_____

_____

_____

_____

_____

FIRST STEPS

DAY 8

I have counsel and sound wisdom; I have insight; I have strength. (Proverbs 8:14 ESV)

Have you ever left on a trip only to realize, five minutes down the road, that you forgot something important? This happens to me more often than I would care to admit. You can almost feel it before you leave. It's as if something is missing. What we need is a checklist.

The Path to Wisdom is fraught with a lot of curves and obstacles. But a checklist will keep you moving forward.

Do we have counsel? No, I don't mean a really good lawyer. Is there a group of friends ready to cheer us and speak Wisdom over our lives? While we're making our way toward Wisdom of our own counsel lets us borrow some from a friend.

Did you pack insight for the journey? Insight is exactly what it sounds like. It's what you get when you take the time to look into something. That's pretty important for any big stuff going on; but it can be equally important for the small stuff. Insight will keep you from missing a vital detail that's hidden in the small matters.

What about strength? How ready are you? It takes effort and energy to arrive anywhere. Travelling can be exhausting under the wrong conditions.

What gives you strength? Is it time alone? Get some. Is it a rowdy evening in the company of your favorite friends? Do that.

We need counsel, insight, and strength to make the trip. It's a recipe for an experience worth remembering. It's an even better list for what will safeguard your life.

Are you missing anything from the list? If so, you're setting yourself up for a struggle. Make this trip toward Wisdom the best it can be.

CHALLENGE: Missing counsel? Book lunch with a friend. Need insight? Find someone who has done it before. Feeling tired? Take a break from the grind and do something today that energizes you.

God, thank you for giving me a checklist that will make this journey better. Help me realize what I need. Help me connect with counsel, gain insight, and gain strength. This journey with you is good.

DAY 9

Do not reprove a scoffer, or he will hate you; reprove a wise man, and he will love you. (Proverbs 9:8 ESV)

Our house is full of small kids. (I think there must be something in the water.) So it seems like one of them is *always* getting into mischief.

How my kids react to discipline is never the same. One day Ethan may accept it with humility, but thirty minutes later act like he didn't deserve it. Jon might grow furious, frustrated, or forlorn when he gets in trouble.

You just don't always know how a kid will respond to correction—but if you're a good parent you still correct them. Why? Because correction leads to Wisdom.

So what about you? How do you respond to correction? I have to admit that younger Nate didn't react very well when someone would correct me. I was hot-headed, arrogant, and not all that receptive much of the time.

It took a shift inside for me to understand the value of correction. If someone takes a moment to offer sincere correction, it's an attempt to make you better. That's a big pivot. It's an entirely different lens.

When you see correction through the right lens you focus on the right thing. Wisdom is the result and love shares the microphone. Both are shouting words that will make you better as you take your next step forward.

CHALLENGE: When was the last time someone lovingly corrected you? Reach out today and tell them, "Thank you".

Father, help me see correction through the right lens. Those who have gathered around me to speak into my life aren't there by accident. Thank you for putting them in my life.

DAY 10

The wise accumulate knowledge—a true treasure; know-it-alls talk too much—a sheer waste. (Proverbs 10:14 MSG)

I love listening to the stories of those who have lived a lot of life. Hearing the details of their journey is like sipping from a well of Wisdom. There is so much to learn there. And it is priceless.

On the flipside one of the hardest lessons for me to learn has been to know when to be quiet. Why? Because I used to think way too highly of what I had to say.

Imagine having someone available to you with the Wisdom to help you navigate precisely where your life is going—only to run over them with your own words when you have the chance to learn. What a waste that would be!

There are times to speak, and times to listen. Wisdom is found in the difference. It's another step forward.

How are you doing when it comes to gathering the valuable lessons others may have to teach? Do you listen? Do you value and treasure the opportunity for what it is?

In a world when there are so many voices competing

for our attention let's resolve not to be one of them all of the time. Let's double down on listening; but also aim our ears at those with something worth listening to. When we hear what's on offer let's see it for what it truly is—something to be treasured.

Learn something today from someone older. Maybe you'll watch a documentary, listen to a podcast, or read a good article. Those are all viable options; but if you can— simply have a conversation. Sit at the feet of your elders and glean something priceless.

CHALLENGE: Ask someone older than you to share their story with you today. Take the time to listen well. Ask questions, but speak little.

God, today I want to learn from the ones you sent before me. Help me hear their story and see how it can help my own. Thank you for the treasured Wisdom that waits in the hearts of the ones who've already walked the Right Path.

DAY 11

When pride comes, then comes disgrace, but with the humble is wisdom. (Proverbs 11:2 ESV)

Every semester when I introduce myself to a new group of students I ask them to call me Nate. Do you know why? Because I am a Nate. Some of them have a hard time with it. So I ask them a question I want to ask you.

Did you know a group of lions is called a pride? It makes sense I suppose. They are remarkable animals. I've never asked one what they thought about the name, but I'd bet he doesn't see a pride. I bet the Head Lion just sees his family and friends. The cool thing about lions is that they are pretty awesome without all of the pomp. In their eyes they are all just lions.

What if, instead of being hung up on the name of a group we find ourselves identifying with, we just decide to be remarkable without all the titles? What if we were just happy being Sally, Felipe, or Rashad?

Humility isn't about shrinking back from what others might think of you. Lions didn't stop eating zebras because

Val Kilmer made a movie about killer lions one time. Lions are just lions. That's how God made them.

Go be you. Be what God made you. You don't have to make a big deal out of it. You're already a big deal. You take another step toward Wisdom when you learn how to rest in that.

What about the title you earned? It's ok if you want to use it. If you're a doctor or lawyer you're a doctor or a lawyer. There's nothing wrong with wanting people to know that part of you. But don't let that become all you are. My kids don't call me Professor Dad. They don't call me Pastor Dad. They just call me Dad. They aren't impressed with me. And you know what? I've learned just how beautiful that really is.

CHALLENGE: Is there a group you belong to or title you possess that you get really excited to tell people about? Go all day without telling anyone.

Father, help me drop the pride around my accomplishments. Help me realize I am more than what I do and what I have done.

DAY 12

Whoever works his land will have plenty of bread, but he who follows worthless pursuits lacks sense. (Proverbs 12:11 ESV)

I grew up no stranger to work. My parents raised me on a small farm along the Arkansas River Valley where my dad grew up. Work was just part of life. Chores always needed to be done. I did an awful lot of complaining. I also did a lot of work.

These days I actually enjoy work. Of course not all work is equal in difficulty. But all work is important.

While not everyone lives in an environment where physical labor is the norm; every step down Wisdom's Trail takes effort. It takes work. Almost none of it comes easily. Ever.

That's a big deal in a world where distractions are normal. They ride around in our pockets, hang on our walls, occupy our nights, and take so many other forms.

Somebody once told me, "How you spend your time is how you'll spend your life." Whoa. It's true. Let's spend it wisely.

What dominated your time last week? What about on a given day? Does the amount of time you spent doing whatever you did reflect what's important to you? Is the life you're living taking you toward Wisdom or somewhere else?

CHALLENGE: Write out a simple schedule of what your day looks like. Be brutally honest.

Lord, show me the heart behind my seconds. Help me really see what I'm spending my time on with honest eyes. Help me make changes that will steer me toward Wisdom.

DAY 13

Careful words make for a careful life; careless talk may ruin every-thing. (Proverbs 13:3 MSG)

When I first started taking my kids hiking I taught them the importance of patience. I told them, "We're not in a hurry." It's a theme we repeat every time we start down the trail. Why? Because when one wrong step could make for a really bad day, it's important to get all of the steps right. It's important to be careful.

Every day is another step. Today is one more move toward your pursuit of a life of Wisdom. God is cheering you even as he encourages you and equips you to take the next step. Here's what I think he is saying to all of us, "we're not in a hurry."

We don't have to rush through what's right in front of us. If everything is urgent nothing is urgent. So save the rushing around for the truly urgent.

Do you know what happens to me when I'm in a hurry? Carefulness goes out the window. Especially where my words are concerned. If I feel like I am under pressure to accomplish something in a hurry, the normal care I try to take with my tongue dwindles quickly. It can happen in the way I grow irritated with a loved one, speak in haste to a friend, or create a misunderstanding with someone I lead on my team or in my classroom. Doubling back to correct the mistake created by hasty words takes a lot more time than taking the time to say careful words in the first place.

The tone your tongue sets says a lot about the way you'll approach Wisdom's Trail. Are you moving forward with care?

CHALLENGE: Use your words to encourage someone today. Speak to them with great care.

Father, guide me in my speech. Let me be an encourager. Help me walk Wisdom's Trail with a careful tongue that loves the people around me.

DAY 14

There is a path before each person that seems right, but it ends in death. (Proverbs 14:12 NLT)

I like giving my kids choices and watching what they do. I think it's important. It's an exercise in good decision making. It helps them learn to pay attention to the details each option offers. One of my favorite questions to ask is, "which way is it back to the car?" Because they've learned the question is coming, they've learned to pay attention. Do they always get the answer right? No, they're just kids. But neither do you and I.

Wisdom's Trail comes with a lot of forks in the road. Places where we have to pick the next step. There are a lot of choices to make. Not all of them lead toward Wisdom. I've spent the better part of two decades helping people sort out the right one.

Some people show up at the fork thinking the right path is the one that feels good. Some have a decidedly different approach. But others don't want to pick a path at all. They keep waiting for God to write the answer on a rock in front of them so it'll be obvious. All because He did that for a guy named Moses one time.

When it comes to taking your next step down Wisdom's Trail it's important to remember where you're going. Wisdom always takes you toward God.

When you reach your next fork in the road you don't have to choose the path that seems right. You can pick the one that *is* right. How will you know? Choose the one that takes you toward the things God cares about. Wisdom will always move you toward hope, joy, peace, forgiveness, and love.

CHALLENGE: What decision do you need to get Wisdom in on today? Which choice moves you toward hope, joy, peace, forgiveness, or love?

God, as I take this next step I want to move toward you. Help me take love in stride, hope along for the ride, and joy with me on this journey. Let me walk in peace and move quickly toward forgiveness.

CAMPFIRE CHAT

What stuck out to you this week?

What are you most excited about?

What are you most concerned about?

What was the most challenging part?

What felt easy?

Where did you feel like God gave you strength for the next step?

Where did you need the help of a friend?

Where did you lend someone else a hand?

Are you being honest with yourself so far?

What are you looking forward to?

FIELD NOTES

_____

_____

_____

_____

_____

_____

_____

_____

_____

_____

THE ASCENT

DAY 15

Without counsel plans fail, but with many advisers they succeed.
(Proverbs 15:22 ESV)

One day I was riding my mountain bike through steep terrain on a brand new trail. I had no idea where I was going. This became really clear when I reached a juncture where several trails converged. I consulted my trail app on my phone. Only my regular go-to app wasn't working. The signal it relied on for service couldn't be found. Thankfully, I had decided to download a different app to try a few days earlier, and this one worked. I was back in business.

Sometimes our plans just don't work out the way we intended. Plans go sideways. Unforeseen circumstances rear their head. While failure is a normal part of life we don't have to chart a course for it.

On Day 2 we talked about taking the step to add wise people to our journey toward Wisdom. If you did that don't disregard what they have to say. If we've only added one person so far it's time to add more.

I have five men I routinely seek advice from. Each

advises me in a different arena of life. I chose them because they are a lot further down the trail than I am. When they speak I listen. When I find them in agreement I REALLY listen.

If your plans keep face-planting it might be time to mix it up. Don't quit; just take it at a different angle. Ask for help. Get a second opinion, (and maybe even a third, fourth, or seventh opinion.) On Wisdom's Trail good friends help point the way.

CHALLENGE: Make a list of the people in your life you go to for advice. Is there an important area you don't have covered? Who can you reach out to for help?

Lord, please place people in my path that will offer honest counsel with wisdom and love. Let me listen well, speak little, and step wise.

DAY 16

Those who listen to instruction will prosper; those who trust the Lord will be joyful. (Proverbs 16:20 NLT)

In my house joy looks a lot like someone set off a bomb in a city made of Lego. Our kids love playing with the small plastic bricks. They build all kinds of things.

One of our boys is meticulous and careful as he builds. He follows the instructions step by step. He doesn't miss a detail. And if he does he quickly doubles back to correct it. For him the process of building is more enjoyable than the end result. One of the boys always builds in a hurry. For him it's not the process of building that excites him. He loves playing with the thing the process creates. As a result he often misses a step and winds up with something that's a bit off, so he has to double back to correct it.

Everyday comes with instructions. I learned a long time ago not to ignore them. Every morning I sit down with my instructions. I pick up my Bible and read one page. That's it. Why? Because I'm not trying to learn more information. I'm looking for my instructions.

There have been days I walked down Wisdom's Trail when I was a lot like my son who heeds the instructions. On those days I did a pretty solid job of paying attention to the instructions God had for me. There have been plenty of other days when I was more like my other son. I was so excited about enjoying the result I wound up with something a bit off.

Life comes with instructions. Learn to trust them. Take each step toward Wisdom with love and confidence. How? Trust the instructions.

CHALLENGE: Read one page in your Bible today. Do it again tomorrow. And the next day. All of the next days. If you miss a day, don't beat yourself up, just don't miss two.

Father, I love Your instructions. Thank You! I pray that as I take it in the truth contained within would steer me ever onward toward Wisdom as I trust in you.

DAY 17

A joyful heart is good medicine, but a crushed spirit dries up the bones. (Proverbs 17:22 ESV)

A few months ago I drove a couple of hundred miles through a blizzard with my best friend to go pick up a puppy. Why? Because I wanted my kids to experience all of the goodness that comes with a new puppy.

Guess what we named her? Joy. She lives up to the name. She brings joy to our house like a rocket fueled by the stuff. It's not uncommon at almost any point in the day for me to look up and see one of my four kids chasing Joy through the house.

It's beautiful, but new puppies are not all hugs and fun. They are still animals. Animals eat. They also do other stuff after they eat. Joy is my daily reminder that I have a choice in how I react to the small stuff and the big stuff. I get to choose my response to the accidents and the opportunities.

How do you react to things? Our reactions are important. I can't control what happens to me. However, I can control my response. I wish I could say that I always ace it.

Your attitude alters your reaction. If you're hopeful you will react in hope. If you're scared you will react in fear.

Your disposition decides your determination. If you have decided to be a compassionate person you will be determined to respond with compassion. If you've decided people are jerks you're going to be determined to be a jerk. There are enough people acting like jerks already. There's not room for you on the roster. Determine to be full of joy.

Joy is a choice. It's the choice you make to let trust in God always move you toward him. It's what Wisdom looks like when adversity shows up big time. It's okay to be bummed sometimes. But if you live there it will crush you. Instead invite joy in. If you feel like chasing something, don't be afraid to chase joy. It's good for you.

CHALLENGE: Resolve today to have a great attitude! Let joy be the guide post you're aiming for all day.

God, help me with my attitude. Help me be determined to follow where joy goes.

DAY 18

God's name is a place of protection—good people can run there and be safe. (Proverbs 18:10 MSG)

When I was about eight years old I got lost in the mountains for a little while. I stumbled through a tear-filled haze for what seemed like hours wishing I could find my Dad. I remember the desperate feeling as if it were yesterday instead of more than thirty years ago. I also remember the way it went away the moment he calmly spoke from nearby, "I'm right here." There's just something about that shift from fear to safety that's hard to forget.

There have been more than a few seasons when he's been a better Dad, than I have son. Even so, when someone says my father's name I don't think about the times when I didn't live up to our name. I think about the moment he spoke from nearby, "I'm right here."

God is a really good Dad. He wants you to know he is close by. He wants you to know he is "right here". There's something about His Name that makes a difference for those on Wisdom's Trail.

Hundreds of years ago people of faith believed God's Name to be so amazing they would get a new pen every time they wrote it. They saw the name of God as something to cherish and honor. They saw an opportunity to gather around His Name with a sincere heart.

Like any good Dad, God has only your best in mind. When you move toward His Name you're moving toward the best of the best. As we keep making steps down Wisdom's Trail remember to step toward all that God has for you. His very best. Remember how close He is. And closer still with every step you take.

CHALLENGE: What was a moment in your life when you felt a shift from fear to safety? Who helped you make the move?

Father, I'm so grateful for the place I find in You. Hard things are always hard. But I can face them with you.

DAY 19

Good sense makes one slow to anger, and it is His glory to overlook an offense. (Proverbs 19:11 ESV)

One night we were all sitting around the table enjoying leftovers for dinner when my son jumped up from the table in a huff and face planted into the tile. It's usually a good idea to let your feet go ahead of your face, but anger can get us all tripped up. You and I are no exceptions.

I've done a lot of really dumb stuff when angry. I've also accomplished some pretty amazing things when angry. Do you know what the difference was? When my anger was justified it fueled me. It was like a surge pushing me toward some wonderful outcome. Unjustified anger though, that's a bit like volunteering to jump off my porch onto my face. It rarely ends well.

You've probably been mad before. Both of us probably will get mad again. Maybe soon. Perhaps even today. Being mad is okay. There are a lot of things around us that would get better if people got mad about them—the right way.

What you and I want to avoid as we take the next step

down Wisdom's Trail is letting anger trip us up. If you're anything at all like me when you're mad you just want to charge ahead. Explosiveness is a great quality in an offensive tackle—not so much in our relationships.

Do you know what I've noticed about anger? It's really unhelpful when it comes too easy. It's also a lot like having two left feet. Be slippery when it comes to anger. Don't let it grab you. Make it work for a living.

Don't be a sucker for anger's sly tricks. Give being offended a hard pass and thumb your nose at a life lived far off of Wisdom's Trail. Anger rooted in pride will take you nowhere you want to be.

CHALLENGE: What was the most angry you've ever been? Why? Was it justified?

God, I need Your help in dealing with my anger. Let me be slow where anger is concerned, quick where patience lives, and consistently moving toward Wisdom.

DAY 20

For who among us can be trusted to be always diligent and honest?
(Proverbs 20:9 MSG)

I've never set off down a trail without stumbling somewhere along the way. It's inevitable. It's also okay. Perfection was never the goal.

We aren't on Perfection's Trail. We are on Wisdom's
Trail. We are moving toward a way of life (one step at a
time) that will guide us in goodness and Wisdom for the
rest of our lives. So how is it going? How do you feel about
where you are?

As we near the last week of our time together on the
trail this is an important step we can't afford to leave out.
So many people give up on their goals because perfection
is so demanding and daunting.

Diligence will keep us moving forward. But we don't do
it with a heart for perfection. We do it with our heart set on
caring about the attempt. Will we ace it? Sometimes. Will
we trip up? You bet.

Obviously neither of us would raise our hands and

declare we want to screw up this journey toward Wisdom. So let's remember to stay really honest about the attempts. If you missed a step on day twelve don't beat yourself about it, just acknowledge the stumble.

God is calling you to keep drawing close to the life He wants for you on Wisdom's Trail. But He isn't counting on your ability to be perfect. He is just asking you to keep taking the next step toward Him.

Today, don't get hung up on your hangups. Today's step down Wisdom's Trail is as simple as it is hard. Today, take a step toward grace for yourself. Let go of that mistake that's been hounding you. Be honest about the ones you've avoided. Move forward.

CHALLENGE: Sit in front of a mirror today and tell yourself out loud about the mistakes you've been hanging onto. Be honest. Love the one looking back at you like God does.

Jesus, sometimes I need help being honest with myself. Sometimes I need help caring about what's going on in my life. Thank you for the grace you give me for both!

DAY 21

Whoever pursues righteousness and kindness will find life, righteousness, and honor. (Proverbs 21:21 ESV)

I'm not much of a chef. If it doesn't involve a grill or a slab of meat it's outside my culinary territory. So I was really surprised one day when my son asked me to bake him a cake for his birthday. But not just any cake. He wanted a ninja cake. I didn't know what that meant, so I made him a chocolate cake and called it a ninja cake. It looked like a cake, and it even tasted like a chocolate cake. We were in business.

I've done a lot of things in my four decades; but baking a cake wasn't on the list. Do you know what I did? I found a recipe. The right recipe tells you what to use, when to use it, and how to do it. And, if you follow the recipe you can get a pretty great cake. It just depends on the recipe.

Wisdom is like that. It's not instant. It's a process. And there is a recipe. As we take our next step together down Wisdom's Trail let's visit two amazing ingredients.

Righteousness is a big word. It's a pretty intimidating

word. Sometimes stuffy people throw it around like it's a badge of perfection. But it doesn't work like that. Righteousness is not something you have, or are, not on your own. It comes from God. It's His. Also, it's something you pursue as Wisdom moves you ever toward Him. But you and I need help to do it. Which is why God gave us kindness.

Kindness is also something you pursue. You move toward it by making decisions that are kind. If you want a life of kindness, be kind.

God knew we didn't have it in us to be righteous. So, He gave us kindness too. The amazing thing is that moving toward one is a lot like moving toward the other. They are in the same direction. They are another step down Wisdom's Trail. They are many steps down Wisdom's Trail.

If you take those steps often enough something pretty amazing will happen. You'll have a really great life. You will just be right. You'll know it because of the path you're on. And because of the way people honor the life you're living.

CHALLENGE: Do something kind for someone today.

Lord, aim me toward kindness today. Let kindness be the step I repeat as I move toward Wisdom and the right path you have for me.

CAMPFIRE CHAT

What stuck out to you this week?

What are you most excited about?

What are you most concerned about?

What was the most challenging part?

What felt easy?

Where did you feel like God gave you strength for the next step?

Where did you need the help of a friend?

Where did you lend someone else a hand?

Are you being honest with yourself so far?

What are you looking forward to?

FIELD NOTES

THE VIEW

DAY 22

Generous hands are blessed hands because they give bread to the poor.
(Proverbs 22:9 MSG)

A few weeks ago we were hiking to a remote waterfall in
the mountains with our kids. Along the way we had to
cross a few streams. Sometimes there were rocks to step on.
Once there was a big tree trunk the boys all scrambled
across. But sometimes we had to help the little ones.

I would reach out my hand and take theirs. And then I
would swing them across— our arms linked together by a
firm grip. But what if I didn't let go? The only way for
them to get where they needed to be was for me to open
my hand and let go.

Generosity means opening your hand. It means letting
go of something you've got in order to make someone
else's life better. It's how you help someone get where they
need to go.

Generosity is one of the most important steps on
Wisdom's Trail. When we learn to open our hands, life
starts getting better for the people around us. Those of us

committed to moving toward God's best for us take a really big step when we acknowledge He has given us the ability to help others get there too.

Far too often people get hung up on money when the talk turns toward generosity. You can be generous with anything. You can be generous with your time by volunteering and listening to a friend. You can be generous with what you know by teaching someone or putting a skill to work. You can be generous with your sweat—try helping someone move—in August.

There are a lot of great ways to be generous. Make a habit out of opening your hand in order to let what you've got help someone get where they need to be. The more you do it the more you want to.

Generosity changes the generous. It makes letting go the next time something to look forward to. Once that becomes the norm you'll go looking for ways to be more generous.

CHALLENGE: Find someone around you with a need and meet it.

Jesus, help me open my hands in generosity. I don't want to be someone who tries to hold on to it all. I want to be someone who helps others get where they need to be.

DAY 23

Surely there is a future, and your hope will not be cut off. (Proverbs 23:18 ESV)

How cool would it be if you could see the future? I'm not talking about looking down the road to dream about flying cars, personal jet packs, and robot maids. This isn't the Jetsons. I am talking about taking a peek down Wisdom's Trail with the certainty good things await you there.

Some days it's hard to lean forward and expect it all to be okay. Other days that kind of outlook comes easy. But here's the thing about living God's best life—hope is always on the table.

Life is not without problems, trials, and pain. It's not without hope either. Hope is what you see when you look down Wisdom's Trail and expect good things await you there.

Hope is a guarantee that you and I didn't write. We don't back it up. But we certainly benefit from it.

Hope is like being able to peek around the corner from a long way off and know there's an opportunity there for something better. Hope is a massive part of each step we take. Hope lies at the heart of our reason for taking off down Wisdom's Trail in the first place.

When everyday circumstances seem a little wild, hope is our best reminder. When the deck seems stacked with failures hope is a galvanizing force. Hope steels you to keep stepping forward. Hope compels you. What are you hoping for?

CHALLENGE: Write down the biggest worry you have in your life right now. Now, what would the situation be like if it got better? That's what hope has to say about it.

Father, thank you for hope. It's too easy to see bad things all around me these days. Let me lean forward with anticipation and hope.

DAY 24

Rescue the perishing; don't hesitate to step in and help. (Proverbs 24:11 MSG)

I was swimming with some friends one day in a narrow channel along the river. We were crossing a spot where people like to jump off the nearby cliffs. As we crossed a boat came roaring into the area right in the middle of our group. All of the guys in the back half of our party had to stop to keep from getting hit. That's when one of my friends cramped up.

In the midst of what was already a hard swim, suddenly my buddy couldn't use one of his legs. It just wouldn't work. He kept going under. He was about to drown.

I had no idea any of this was happening until I was just about to leave the water. I turned around and saw my friend in trouble. I saw other friends struggling to help him. I didn't hesitate. Somehow I found a new gear and made it back to them in time to help take my friend to safety.

I wish I could say that I always tried to help those in

trouble. I wish it always worked out the way it did with my friend in the river. Unfortunately there have been times when I saw someone in trouble and hesitation got the best of me.

Trouble isn't always immediate. Sometimes trouble unfolds in an instant. Some troubles lie in wait for decades.

The next step down Wisdom's Trail means taking a step toward someone in trouble. Who do you know whose life is on the line? Who do you know whose marriage is in dire straits? Is there someone close to you piling up mistakes that are sure to crash down around them? Don't hesitate.

If you saw someone you loved drowning you wouldn't just stand around. You would help. Someone near you is drowning. They are in over their head. They can't do it by themselves. Jump in.

CHALLENGE: Someone in your life needs a friend who won't hesitate. Find them. Help. Don't wait.

Father, I don't want to hesitate. Help me be someone who helps. Open my eyes to those in my life facing some real trouble and help me make a difference there.

DAY 25

A word spoken at the right time is like gold apples in silver settings. (Proverbs 25:11 MSG)

I looked up just in time to scream, "Noooooooo!" Just as my son was about to step into the street. My heart pounded. It had only taken a fraction of a moment as I helped one of his siblings, but my lapse in attention was loaded with the potential for disaster.

Words are precious. Words are valuable. Words that help those around us are so important. And the right word spoken at the right time can be more powerful and more important than we can begin to imagine.

If my kids are tuned into something else I have to say the words that change their focus. Usually I say, "Look at me." Sometimes I have to say their name. The right words will influence focus. Sometimes I need to hear the right words to shift my own focus.

Every step down Wisdom's Trail takes focus. None of us will blunder our way into a life of Wisdom on accident. It takes moving there on purpose. As we've already mentioned—what someone says to us can make a big difference. By now you get that.

Today, let's shift our focus. Let's focus on saying the right word at the right time for the right person in our life.

This will mean being tuned in. We will have to really pay attention. We'll have to fight to avoid distractions—even good ones.

Resolve today to whisper an encouraging word to a friend. If they don't hear you get louder. Don't be a jerk about it. Be focused.

By now you're sharing Wisdom's Trail with people who mean the world to you. Say something priceless. What you say may make all of the difference for them today.

CHALLENGE: Tell someone what they need to hear today. If you don't know what that is just tell them how important they are to you.

Lord, I don't want to miss the chance to say something that will help someone I love today. Help me bring out words that make a difference today.

DAY 26

Do you see a man who is wise in his own eyes? There is more hope for a fool than for him. (Proverbs 26:12 ESV)

What do you see when you look in the mirror? Who do you see? What is your response to you?

Answers probably register all across the spectrum. Some have reached a place of maturity and carry a pretty honest assessment of the one staring back from the silvery surface. Others look into the smooth reflection and have a tough time seeing more than the flaws that persist. Perhaps you see someone who makes you mad. Or maybe you're regretful when you look into your own eyes. What about someone who is wise?

As we now near the end of our time together on this stretch of Wisdom's Trail we need to take stock of something important. You and I don't decide how far we are down the trail. While there are important signs that show us how far we've come, and there are great reminders drawing us on—we never get there. We never reach the end of the road where Wisdom is concerned. Because

Wisdom is always calling us to take another step, we abandon it if we decide we've gone far enough.

Wisdom's Trail is full of grandiose panoramas, striking vistas, and a world of things to learn and marvel at. There are an awful lot of rest stops, places to camp, and sites to take in the sights. But there aren't any destinations. There are no arrivals.

We never arrive at Wisdom, because it isn't a place you go. Wisdom is a way you live your life as you pursue all of the goodness God intends for you along the way. We could all do with a little more Wisdom.

Take a moment today to remind yourself of just how far you've come. And then promise yourself you will keep on going.

CHALLENGE: Go to your favorite place outside. As you soak it in, write down a few things you've learned about Wisdom over the last three weeks.

Father, I celebrate how far you've brought me down Wisdom's Trail. I am excited about where you're taking me next. Thank you for every step.

DAY 27

Iron sharpens iron, and one man sharpens another. (Proverbs 27:17 ESV)

My boys went into the nearby forest to collect firewood one day while we were camping. My oldest got the hatchet and decided to gather some bigger sticks. Pretty soon he came back beaming with pride and a sizable chunk of wood.

Not to be outdone, his younger brother decided to do the same. Only, he didn't really know how. Pretty soon I found him trying to chop up rocks. I cringed a bit as I took the tool away. Looking at it up close I could see the once pristine blade was a mess of nicks and blunted spots.

Blunt blades cut little. They make a mess. They make the work more difficult. Every step down Wisdom's Trail is a little harder if you've lost your edge.

Gathering a group of trusted individuals around you to share Wisdom's Trail is a vital part of the journey we've worked on previously. Today, I want us to focus on the importance of giving each other an edge.

The value of friends cannot be overstated. Building

close relationships is essential. The closer we are the better the edge. It takes someone close to see how sharp you really are.

Advice is awesome. Learning from one another is a critical skill to have. Counsel comes with the job called friend. Do all of that for someone even as they do it for you. And then go one step further.

The most valuable relationships in my life are the ones who help me keep my edge. No one is closer than my wife. She helps me stay sharp. She reminds me when something won't bring about the result I was hoping for.

I've had some amazing friends join me on the trail too. Sometimes I can tell my edge is slipping so I'll ask for help. Then there are times when they notice before I do and they'll tell me what they see. We all need a close friend who can help us keep our edge. The closer they are, the better they see.

CHALLENGE: What have you been holding back from the ones sharing the trail with you? Invite someone trustworthy a little closer today. Tell them something you've never talked about before.

Father, thank you for the ones who keep me sharp. I'm not sure where I'd be without them.

DAY 28

Better is a poor man who walks in his integrity than a rich man who is crooked in his ways. (Proverbs 28:6 ESV)

I'm always a bit disheartened when I encounter broken glass while on a hike. I don't like it when someone shows disrespect for the trail. It demonstrates a disregard for who may follow. It demonstrates lacking integrity.

Integrity is an important waypoint on Wisdom's Trail. Your integrity is how you walk when no one is there to see you take your next step.

Integrity compels you to stay on the right path. Each and every step we take comes with an opportunity to go somewhere else. Sometimes we will misstep. And if you and I aren't careful we'll leave little pieces of ourselves behind.

God collects broken people. He wouldn't want either of us to look back and focus on the moments when our integrity shattered. Instead, take a moment to thank Him for getting you to where you are in one piece. You are who you are because God took all of those missed moments and rolled them up into a grace-covered version of you.

On your next step don't leave behind what you learned from your mistakes. Take it with you. The value on offer where integrity is the teacher is better than anything else you will encounter along the way.

What have you learned from your mistakes? Let it prepare you for the next step.

CHALLENGE: What did you learn from a past mistake that can help you with today's difficulties?

God, thank you for grace. I know I am where I am and I am who I am because you collected me in the moments when I missed the right step. Help me take what you've done and learn from it.

CAMPFIRE CHAT

What stuck out to you this week?

What are you most excited about?

What are you most concerned about?

What was the most challenging part?

What felt easy?

Where did you feel like God gave you strength for the next step?

Where did you need the help of a friend?

Where did you lend someone else a hand?

Are you being honest with yourself so far?

What are you looking forward to?

FIELD NOTES

_____

_____

_____

_____

_____

_____

_____

_____

_____

_____

THE SUMMIT

DAY 29

Pride brings a person low, but the lowly in spirit gain honor. (Proverbs 29:23 MSG)

I was flying down the trail on my bike. Everything was going right. I was moving like I had been riding all of my life—even though I had only been at it for a few months. I was feeling pretty good—too good.

As I came to the top of hill I stopped to take in what was next rather than roll in blind. Before me the trail dropped about twenty feet with a pretty steep grade. At the bottom was a little creek a few feet wide before the trail ascended another twenty feet at an equally steep angle. I had never attempted anything like that before.

I positioned myself and my bike. I inched forward and then momentum propelled me. I hit the descent without slowing at all, rolled right through the creek at maximum speed, and made it almost all the way to the top before everything went wrong.

Rather than slow down I had leaned too far back on my bike. In the brief moment it took to transition from down to up I hadn't changed my posture enough. Suddenly my bike was not under me anymore. It continued up the incline as I came off and careened into the hard packed dirt. My confidence had outpaced my skill set.

We all face moments when we are brought in check. Reality sets in. We weren't quite ready for that thing we attempted. Or maybe we should have gone at it in a slightly different way.

You and I can't afford to let pride set our path on Wisdom's Trail. Pride will always set you up for a fall. Falling hurts.

Remember to face each new twist and turn for what it is, something new. Rather than roll in at max speed take a moment to recount what you've learned. This far down Wisdom's Trail you have a lot to reflect on.

CHALLENGE: Remind yourself of a moment when you incorrectly assumed you were ready for your next step. What did you learn there?

Jesus, I'm thankful for moments that teach me what you want me to learn along the way. Thank you for picking me back up when I fall.

DAY 30

I am weary, God, but I can prevail. (Proverbs 30:1 NIV)

Do you know what I hear again and again from my friends who run marathons? Somewhere around the middle weariness sets in. Muscles truly begin to feel the weight of what is being asked of them. Desire for rest creeps up. Fatigue hounds their every step. Do you know what else they all say? They kept going.

There's a moment in every journey when the tedium of the terrain sets in. Excitement for the attempt wears thin. The sights don't pop and dazzle quite like they did in the beginning. Each step becomes a little more difficult. Wisdom's Trail is no different.

I hit a season of weariness last year—and it was both frightening and dumbfounding in its scope. But I didn't quit. I thought about it. I talked about it with my friends. The conversation went a bit like this, "What if I didn't do this anymore?"

Fatigue isn't a fake thing whether we're talking about a physical endeavor or an emotional event. Weariness is real.

Eventually, if you take enough steps the culmination of them begins to wear at you—even though you were going somewhere amazing.

Maybe weariness took a swing at you a while back and now you know what to expect. Or, it could be that it's about to creep up on you in earnest for the first time. Maybe you can already feel it seeping in at the edge of your effort.

Do you know what's really good for weariness? Rest. Take a break. Sometimes the best next step is not to take a step at all. Hang your hammock in a place that refreshes you and spend some time there.

Get some rest, but don't quit. Don't stay where you stopped. Talk to God about what you're doing. I find that he is usually already waiting where I stop to rest. Tell him what you need. And when you feel the needle shift away from weary, move on. You will prevail.

CHALLENGE: Schedule a break today. Don't fill it with responsibilities. Fill it with rest. Read a book you've put off. Take a nap. Take a drive through the mountains. Rest. Talk to God about it.

God, I am tired and weary. I am ready for rest. I know you want me healthy for the long haul. Thank you for helping me change my rhythm and get back some energy for the next step.

DAY 31

Open your mouth for the mute, for the rights of all who are destitute.
(Proverbs 31:8 ESV)

When we began having children we decided we wouldn't stop doing the things we like to do outdoors just because we had babies. That meant we would still hike, fish, and camp regularly. But we had to figure out how to do it with a baby and still be responsible parents. Each time our family has grown we've had to learn it all over again.

Early on a great solution presented itself. We would put the baby in a small device meant to protect them and hold them close. We literally carried the baby everywhere we went as they moved with us step for step.

As you move down Wisdom's Trail you're going to cross paths with a lot of people. Many of them have no idea which way to go. And they don't even know how to ask for help. The circumstances of their lives have stolen their voice.

Look out for the ones who can't make it on their own. Speak up for them. Sometimes this will mean simply giving good directions. There will be moments when they may need a hand up. You might have to help drag them out of trouble. One of the best steps you will ever take down Wisdom's Trail is the one where you learn to use the steps you've already made to make someone else's life better.

Maybe up until now you thought this journey was about you. It's not. God didn't beckon you toward him so He can have you all to himself. He wants you to turn around and help the one behind and beside you. Every time your strength makes a difference for someone who can't do it you're showing them how good God is.

Become a voice for the voiceless. Be a strong hand for the weak ones. Take an extra step toward the one struggling to take theirs. As you help someone else move down the right path your own path will be made so much better.

CHALLENGE: Look around today. Who can't do what they need to do. How can you help them? Don't just think about it. Do it.

Father, forgive me for sitting on the sidelines. Help me see who needs help. Help me move toward them. Give me the strength to lend them what they need. Let them see how good you are through what you've shown me to do.

BACK TO THE TRAILHEAD

Not every hike ends where it begins. But every journey wraps up somewhere. I hope the last thirty-one days together have made a difference.

I hope you have stories to tell about things you've learned. I hope you've got some friends that can share theirs. You've finished thirty-one steps toward a lifetime of Wisdom. That's not a small thing. You should celebrate.

You should also know by now that you're just getting started. Maybe you're already planning the next adventure. Hopefully you feel equipped to go at it with gusto.

My big hope for you all along has been that this journey together would kickstart your appetite for more. God always has another step for you. Not because He's trying to squeeze more out of you, but because he always has so much more to offer.

Keep taking steps toward Him. Keep moving your life in the direction where love leads first and Wisdom guides every step. God wants all of his best for all of your days.

There are sweeping panoramas waiting. Places where you'll see what you've never seen before. There are twists and turns that will help you revisit where you've already been from a new angle. Always be ready to soak it in, share it often, and take another step.

I'm excited about how far we've come together. I'm encouraged by where you're going next. You've got so many steps left in you.

Wisdom is your constant companion. It is, afterall, Wisdom's Trail you're walking on. Enjoy the journey. Pray big prayers. Dream big dreams. Take the next big step. I'll see you at the end.

Until then, Godspeed.

Nate

BONUS CHAPTER

The following is an excerpt from "Learn Love Live: The Story God Wants for Your Life" coming January 4, 2022.

FALLING DOWN

We all fall.

We all fall sometimes. I know I have. Sometimes it's funny and sometimes it hurts, but a fall is a fall. One time I fell going up some steps in front of about a thousand people I was getting ready to talk to. That was cool. One time I fell playing basketball and had to have surgery on my knee a few weeks later. That was not cool.

Every fall is different, but rarely are they good. We all experience falls. It can be hilarious when people fall, but not always. You know you laugh when you see it happen. You know you do.

Men and women fall differently too don't they? When guys fall there's no ignoring it. It's like a train wreck. It's probably because we're loud or big or both. It's like smacking the ground smashes all the testosterone into our face and we hop back up and act like we just scored a touchdown. Like it energizes us or something.

Ladies, when you fall you act like nothing happened! Like you decided to hit a random yoga pose while you were walking to your car or something. Have you ever seen a woman slip on the ice? It's like in the split second following she's decided to try out for the Olympic Winter Games. It's a testament to the grace God gave you that you can pull it off so well.

Let's face it. Sometimes a fall can be funny. But seeing someone fall isn't always funny is it? Especially as a parent. Have you ever watched your kid fall? Of course you have! How did it feel? It was awesome right? No! No one ever calls their wife and says, "Baby, I just watched little Timmy faceplant into the kitchen tile. It was amazing!" No, that doesn't happen.

A couple of years ago our middle son Jon was at home with Jamie. While she was working hard doing what moms do, he climbed up on a couch—and then jumped off—right onto a toy—with his face! Ouch! But that kind of thing happens. It doesn't make my wife a bad mom that Jon decided to test gravity.

Being a boy-dad guarantees a few things in my life. It means I will never be far from a surplus of Legos. It means there will almost always be someone fighting, yelling, eating, or pooping in my house. It also means there will be falls, boo-boos, and blood.

Jon fell on a pen on New Year's Eve when he was one. It went right into his mouth and stabbed deep into the tissue. He screamed, and choked, and bled and I completely freaked out. My wife did not. She was calm and cool as she got a popsicle and made our son suck on it which promptly stopped the bleeding. Wonder Woman doesn't panic at the sight of blood.

A few months later Jon was wrestling with Ethan when he went face first into the arm of a small wooden chair typically reserved for "time out". On this occasion the chair dished out a different kind of punishment. It busted his forehead open just above his eyebrow. It was nasty, so we were off to the urgent care center nearby.

It turned out not to be a big deal, but I don't like taking chances when it involves my child's head and blood. Jon was cool about the whole thing. Way cooler than me. He must get that from Wonder Woman. In fact, as he lay on the examination table talking to the nurses they asked his name. He replied with the utter seriousness you can only expect from a two-year-old, "I'm Batman." They believed him.

Then there was our latest in a long line of spills and falls that mostly didn't make this list. It happened just a couple of weeks ago. One Friday afternoon Jamie met Ethan and I at the local theater after running some errands, so we could all enjoy the latest summer superhero movie.

A slight thunderstorm had swept through the area during the movie, so the parking lot was wet as we were leaving. Ethan was climbing into the back of my SUV to get buckled into his chair when his wet shoes slid out from under him on the metal trim. He upended in slow motion. His feet seemed to go up as his head went back and down. He landed squarely on the back of his head. His six-year-old noggin taking the full force of the impact.

By the time I made it around the car to get to him blood was already pooling on the pavement beneath his head. He was crying uncontrollably. I was scared. I asked him if he knew his name and he did. I asked if he knew how old he was, and he knew that too. I asked him if I could give his little brothers all his Legos. He said, "No way!" Trying to believe the best I wrapped his head in a blanket, put him in his mom's van, and we drove to the Emergency Room a few blocks away.

I carried him inside to the receptionist's desk. I hadn't had time to notice what either of us looked like before walking in. But the size of everyone's eyes as we passed by said enough. Then I saw my reflection in the glass in the reception area. I was covered in Ethan's blood. So was he.

Apparently walking into the emergency room with a child covered in blood causes things to move a little faster than I've been accustomed to on previous trips to the ER. Within a couple of minutes, we were being taken to the back. The doctors were awesome. The injury turned out to be minor, and the stay was short. I think we were there less than an hour.

Maybe it's just the hillbilly nature in me—but the way I learned falling was bad was by falling. Because it's in our nature to test our limits. To try and fail. To mess up. As a parent I know this. And as a son I know this. I'm learning to live on both sides of that coin. I'm just crazy enough to believe God had this all figured out a long time ago. Because he is the best of parents.

He knew we would fall. He knew we would mess up. I don't believe he sits back and urges us to fail. I don't think he is at all happy about it. But he doesn't bubble wrap us either. God, in his infinite wisdom knew we would mess up a lot and it hasn't changed how much he cares about us.

With our boys, and our rough and tumble lifestyle, we've adopted a saying in our house:

"What do we do when we fall down?"
    "We get back up!"

One time we were with Ethan at the park. He was climbing something a little beyond his means, but he had climbed it a few times. I had helped him previously, but this time I was standing at the top urging him on. In hindsight this was a terrible idea. I had my phone out ready to snap some pics of my son conquering this climbing-thing and then it happened. He fell.

Time slowed down and simultaneously gravity sped up and I watched helplessly as my little boy dropped more than five feet to land flat on his back on the gravel.

If you're a parent you know what I was feeling at that moment. It was gut wrenching! It was miserable. This person I love so much, this person I am supposed to protect, He had just fell. He was hurt. He was crying.

This is exactly what God experiences regularly with us. He made us, and he loves us more than anything. How often does he watch us make these terrible choices that lead to a fall?

Let me ask you a question: How many of you are human? No, that's not a trick question. I don't think we have any robots reading this. We were all born human beings. Raise your hand if you were born a human. Go ahead. Do it. Now look around. If you see anyone else raising their hand, ask them how they are liking the book.

The Bible has a letter in it written from this guy Paul to some friends of his in Rome. Paul's friends were guys like us. People who knew what it was like to fall. To mess up big time. So, Paul wrote something incredible. He said, "Everyone trips up; we all fall short of God's glorious standard."

Let me let you in on a deep theological secret. "Everyone" in the Greek means *everyone*. That's all of us. We have all messed up. Like my son reaching for something beyond his means. We have all fallen short. Of what?!? Of God's Glorious Standard.

Every time we fall it hurts. It causes pain. It causes suffering and repercussions. Sometimes we are in pain because of our own falling and failures. Sometimes we are in pain because of the failures of someone else. Sometimes someone else falls and we get caught in the mess, but we all fall short and we all fall down.

So, what do we do about it? "What do we do when we fall down?" "We get back up!"

Returning to the story of Ethan falling at the park…. You know, because you might need to hear more about how terrible of a parent I am sometimes!

Remember, he fell five feet and landed flat on his back on the tiny gravel that filled the playground area. All of this happened right in front of me. Right within my reach. While, of all things, I was busy getting ready to snap a pic of him on my phone.

Instinctively, I dropped my phone. I jumped off the top of this playground thing at the park. I reached down, and scooped Ethan up, and held him close. He was crying. He was gasping for breath because it had all been knocked out of him. But he composed himself after a couple of seconds in my arms.

I looked at his little tear-filled eyes. And do you know what I asked him? That's right! "What do we do when we fall down?"

He gasped, "We……. get…… back……. Up."

It's hard to get back up when you're hurt. It's hard for you and me to get back up when we fall. So often we feel this thing inside of us best described as missed potential. We feel this thing inside telling us we have missed something.

Ultimately God's love is like a parent throwing caution to the wind to reach down and scoop up a hurting child. Some of you of have fallen hard, and you've started seeing *yourself* as the thing that trips you up.

Some days it takes real effort to see past all the mistakes

I've made in my life. It is so easy to see myself and my failures "as the same thing". Do you look in the mirror and see an addiction, a failure, or a persistent lack of self-worth? Do you look in the mirror but only see the things making you fall?

You must know God doesn't see you that way at all. God doesn't see a problem to be solved. God doesn't see a project to be managed. God doesn't see a failure to be fixed. God sees a son or a daughter to be rescued.

Have you fallen? He can reach you. Have you messed up? He can sort you out. Have you felt like you fell so far that help is out of reach and hope is out of sight? Look up, reach up, God's got you.

What do we do when we fall down? We get back up. God helps us.

ABOUT THE AUTHOR

Nathan King lives with his family in Arkansas. You can often find him riding his bike off the side of a mountain, building something with his hands, or catching the latest superhero movie with his family. He also serves as an adjunct professor at his alma mater Arkansas Tech University. He and Jamie have the distinct privilege of serving as pastors at New Life Church in Clarksville, AR. You can find him online at www.nathanking.com or in his neighborhood walking his dog. For speaking inquiries contact help@nathanking.com.